This book is dedicated to my
high school creative writing teacher, Mr. Karnes.
Thank you for encouraging me to believe in myself.

Designed by Flowerpot Press
www.FlowerpotPress.com
CHC-0810-0521 • 978-1-4867-2108-5
Made in China/Fabriqué en Chine

Drip the Raindrop

Written by Cara Moyers   Illustrated by Charlie Astrella

I'm Drip the raindrop
and I'm always nonstop.
I'm constantly moving about.

My adventure starts subtle,
on the ground in a puddle,
as I wait for the sun to come out.

It's pink in the sky
as the sun starts to rise;
bright, beaming rays start to show.

Just as I thought,
the puddle gets hot
and up into the air I go!

Now I'm water vapor!
I'm lighter than paper
in a process called evaporation.

It's amazing to see
the whole world below me,
all the trees and the seas and the nations.

As I cool down,
I jump into a cloud
and say, "Hey" to my H_2O friends.

We get closer together
and as we become weather,
I turn back into a raindrop again.

In a whirlwind of wonder,
the lightning and thunder
signal us drops to get ready.

At the start of the storm,
we begin taking form
as the dark, puffy clouds get heavy.

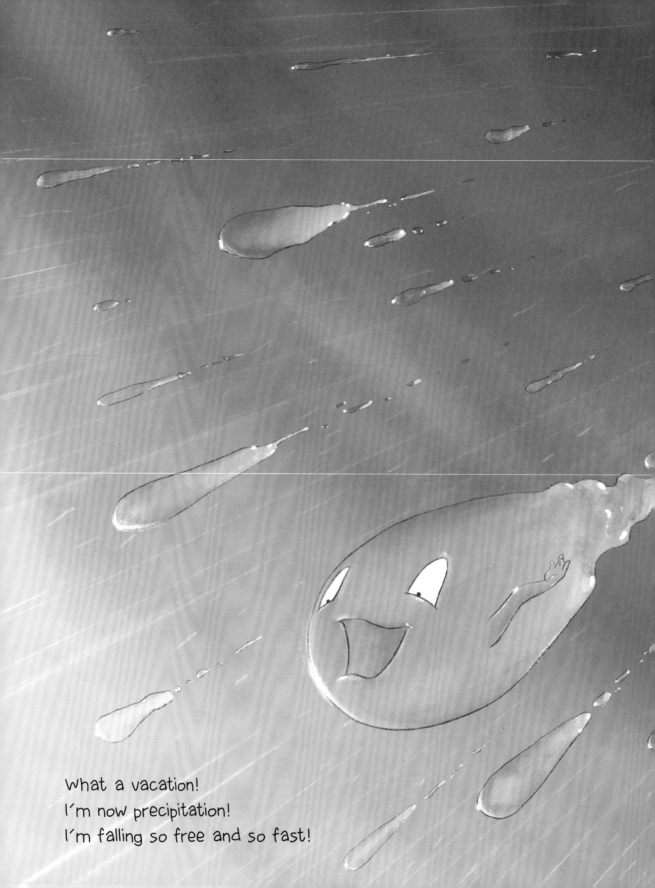

What a vacation!
I'm now precipitation!
I'm falling so free and so fast!

I run down a mountain,
splash off like a fountain,
landing back in my puddle at last.

Don't worry friend,
this isn't the end.
The water cycle never stops.

I'm water, you see,
so lucky for me,
I'll always be Drip the raindrop!

Drip's Adventures Never End

Now that you've read about Drip's journey, take a look at some of the other adventures Drip can go on as a raindrop. These adventures are all part of the water cycle! The water cycle describes the way in which water is constantly changing form from a liquid (when Drip is in his puddle) to a gas (when Drip evaporates and goes into the sky) to a solid (when Drip becomes snow or ice). It's called a cycle because water changes forms over and over again but never leaves or stops.

<u>CONDENSATION</u>: After Drip becomes a gas, he goes higher and higher into the air, eventually cooling down and becoming a liquid again. Once he's a water droplet, he will meet up with his friends and they will form clouds and fog.

<u>TRANSPIRATION</u>: When Drip is released from the leaves of a plant, it is called transpiration. Plants need water like Drip to help them grow and stay healthy, so they suck up Drip and his friends from the ground. When the trees have had enough, they will release Drip into the air.

<u>EVAPORATION</u>: When Drip is part of a body of water or even just in his puddle, he will stay there until he evaporates. Evaporation occurs when the sun heats Drip and his friends up enough until they eventually become a gas.

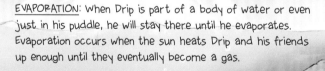

<u>GROUNDWATER FLOW</u>: Even when Drip is underground, he is still on the move. Drip and his friends move underground so they can eventually find a body of water. Usually Drip's journey underground is very slow.

SUBLIMATION: When Drip is snow, he can sometimes be turned back into a gas called water vapor without even becoming a liquid. Through the intense heat of the sun, some snow will absorb enough heat to become a gas.

PRECIPITATION: When clouds get too heavy from all the water droplets they're holding, they will release Drip and his friends in the form of rain, snow, sleet, or hail, depending on the temperature.

SNOWMELT: When Drip falls from a cloud as snow, he will eventually melt and return to a body of water as runoff or go underground.

RUNOFF: When Drip falls from a cloud as rain, there are a few places he can end up. If he lands in a body of water, he will stay in that body of water. But if Drip ends up on sloped land, he will become runoff and do his very best to slide back down to a body of water.

INFILTRATION: Sometimes when Drip falls to the ground as rain, he will eventually go even deeper into the ground, infiltrating the earth's surface. When he is underground, he is called groundwater. In the ground, Drip can provide plants with the water they need to survive.

ACTIVITIES TO TRY AT HOME

CLOUD IN A BOTTLE

To see the effects of evaporation and condensation at home, all you need is a clear water bottle, an ice cube, hot water, and some help from an adult.

1. Have an adult help you fill the water bottle with hot water.

2. Leave the hot water in the water bottle for about ten seconds. Then pour half of the water out.

3. Carefully place an ice cube on top of your water bottle. The ice cube should cool the water vapor in the bottle, creating a cloud.

EVAPORATION EXPERIMENT

. . . .

Evaporation is an invisible process. We can't see water turning into water vapor. But you can see the effects of evaporation. All you need for this experiment is a camera, four clear glasses, and four coasters.

1. Fill each glass to the top with water.

2. Place one glass on top of a coaster in a very sunny place. A windowsill is a great option.

3. Place one glass on top of a coaster on a table somewhere where very little sunlight will shine on it.

4. Place one glass on top of a coaster inside of a closet where no light will shine on it.

5. Place the last glass on a coaster in the refrigerator.

6. Take a picture of each glass once they are all in place.

7. Come back to each glass over the course of the next few days and take a picture each day.

8. Compare the glasses and the amount of water in each one at the end of your experiment to see how different areas affect evaporation. Look at the photos you took to see how each glass changed along the way.

GLOSSARY

CLOUD — A collection of water droplets in the sky

CONDENSATION — When water cools down and changes from a gas to a liquid

EVAPORATION — When water turns to gas

FOG — A thick cloud of water droplets closer to Earth's surface

GROUNDWATER — Water that is underground

H_2O — The scientific name for water

HAIL — Balls of ice that come down during thunderstorms

ICE — The solid form of water

INFILTRATION — When water goes deep into the ground

OCEAN — Where most of the Earth's water is in the form of salt water

PRECIPITATION — When water falls from the clouds

RAIN — A form of precipitation

RUNOFF — Water that runs off the Earth's surface

SLEET — A form of precipitation that is a mixture of rain and snow

SNOW — Solid form of rain that occurs at or below 32°F/0°C

SNOWMELT — When snow melts and becomes runoff

SUBLIMATION — When snow skips the liquid stage of water and becomes a gas

TRANSPIRATION — When plants release water into the air

VAPOR — The gas form of water

WATER CYCLE — The cycle that water goes through in which it can be a solid, a liquid, or a gas

In an effort to improve our world and in collaboration with Trees for the Future (TREES), a tree will be planted for every book purchased. Our plant a tree partnership is a way for us to assist TREES in their efforts to heal the environment and alleviate poverty for smallholder farmers in impoverished countries. To learn more about TREES, visit trees.org.